POWERSKATEBOARDING™

Skateboarding Tricks and Techniques

Justin Hocking

The Rosen Publishing Group's
PowerKids Press™
New York

For Matt and Sean

Safety gear, including helmets, wrist guards, knee pads, and elbow pads, should be worn while skateboarding. Do not attempt tricks without proper gear, instruction, and supervision.

Published in 2006 by The Rosen Publishing Group, Inc.
29 East 21st Street, New York, NY 10010

Copyright © 2006 by The Rosen Publishing Group, Inc.

All rights reserved. No part of this book may be reproduced in any form without permission in writing from the publisher, except by a reviewer.

First Edition

Editor: Melissa Acevedo
Book Design: Elana Davidian

Photo Credits: Cover © Joe McBride/Getty Images; pp. 4 (top left), 7 (left and top right), 8, 11–12, 15–16, 19–20 Nancy Opitz; p. 4 (bottom left) © Corbis; p. 4 (right) © Fotopic/Index Stock Imagery; p. 7 (bottom right) © Kevin Dodge/Masterfile.

Library of Congress Cataloging-in-Publication Data

Hocking, Justin.
Skateboarding tricks and techniques / Justin Hocking.
    p. cm. — (Power skateboarding)
Includes bibliographical references and index.
ISBN 978-1-4358-3812-3
1. Skateboarding—Juvenile literature. I. Title. II. Series.

GV859.8.H627 2006
796.22—dc22
                              2004022497

Manufactured in the United States of America

Contents

1. Learning to Skateboard — 5
2. Safety — 6
3. Foot Position and Pushing Technique — 9
4. How to Turn — 10
5. Manuals — 13
6. Ollies — 14
7. Frontside 180 Ollies — 17
8. Pop Shove-Its — 18
9. Kick Flips — 21
10. Putting It All Together — 22
    Glossary — 23
    Index — 24
    Web Sites — 24

Skateboarding is a good form of exercise and a great way to make friends! *Top left:* A skater rolls down a ramp. *Bottom left:* These skaters have bonded over their shared interest in skateboarding. *Right:* To pop a wheelie like the skater above, you need balance.

Learning to Skateboard

Skateboarding is a popular activity today. There are almost 10 million skaters in the United States alone! Skaters can be seen in TV commercials, on billboards, in the movies, and even in video games. If you are thinking about getting into skateboarding, there are many great reasons to start. One of the main reasons people skateboard is because it is fun and they enjoy doing different tricks. Riding around and doing tricks on a skateboard can give you feelings of freedom and accomplishment.

This book will teach you how to do several beginner tricks. It will also give you some tips on how to land these moves. However, along the way you will discover your own **techniques** for doing tricks because everyone does each trick a little differently. Another great thing about skateboarding is that it lets you **express** yourself and skate with your own style.

Safety

Skateboarding has been proven to be as safe as football or basketball. However, if you spend lots of time skateboarding, you will get hurt on occasion. That is just part of being a skateboarder. There are steps you can take to keep yourself safe, though. The most important thing to remember is to always wear a helmet to keep your head from getting hurt. You should also always wear knee pads and elbow pads.

Another important way to avoid getting hurt is to move at your own pace. Skateboarding is not about showing off or trying to **compete** with other skaters. It is just about having fun and being the best skater you can be. Learn how to turn and just ride around first before trying harder tricks. Spend as much time as you need on each new trick. That way you will feel comfortable on your skateboard when you try harder moves and tricks.

Always remember to move at your own pace and keep your balance, like the skater above.
Top right: This skater knows that wearing safety gear is important to keep from getting hurt.
Bottom right: These skaters know skateboarding is more fun when you follow safety rules.

regular-footed stance

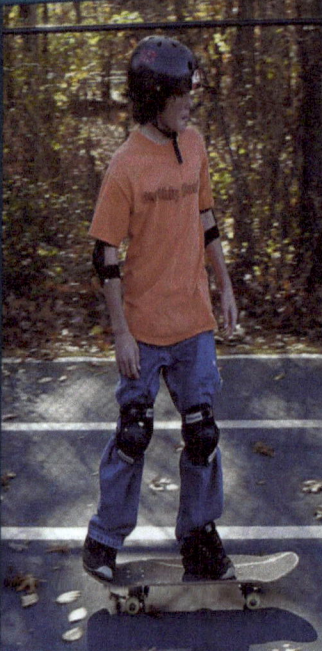

In the regular-footed stance you stand with your left foot in front of your right foot on your board. The skater in the picture above is regular footed.

goofy-footed stance

The skater above is standing on his board with his right foot in front of his left one. This is called the goofy-footed stance.

pushing off

To push off on your skateboard, place one of your feet firmly on the board, facing the front. Push the board forward with your back foot as shown above.

Foot Position and Pushing Technique

There are two different types of stances, or ways of standing on a skateboard. Skaters who stand with their left foot forward on a skateboard are regular footed. Skaters who stand with their right foot forward are called goofy footed. Either way you stand, your front foot should point forward and turn out a little. It should rest just above your front **trucks**. Your back foot should sit straight across on your **tail**, just above your back trucks.

Use your back foot to push your board. Using your front foot will make keeping your balance harder. When you take your back foot off to push, turn your front foot so that your toes point toward the front of your board. This will make balancing on the board easier as you push. Once you finish pushing and put your back foot back on the board, you can turn your front foot sideways again.

When you first start skating, you should try out both stances just to see which one is more comfortable for you. Where you place your feet on the board is very important.

How to Turn

Now that you know how to push, it is time to learn how to turn. To do a **frontside** turn, lean toward the back of your skateboard and put your weight on your heels. To do a **backside** turn, lean toward the front of your board and put your weight on your toes. Skate down the street or sidewalk, practicing turns and getting comfortable on your board until you get the hang of it.

Another type of turn is called the kick turn. Kick turns allow you to make sharper, quicker turns. When you do a kick turn, the front of the board lifts as you **swivel** the board around on your back wheels. To start a kick turn, press down on the tail of the board with your back foot. Lift your front wheels completely off the ground. Use your feet and hips to spin the front of the board around toward the direction in which you want to turn.

> If you are regular footed and do a frontside turn, your board will turn left. If you are goofy footed, your board will turn right. The opposite is true for a backside turn. Goofy-footed skaters will turn left while doing a backside turn. Regular-footed skaters' boards will turn right.

Kick Turn

1  To start the kick turn, push off on your board and roll forward. Notice where the skater's feet are on the board.

2  Raise the front of the board into a low wheelie with your back foot.

3  Move the front of the board in the direction you want to go. Drop the front of the board to the ground and keep skating.

Frontside Turn

 After pushing off with your back foot, lean toward the back of your board. Put all your weight on your heels in order to turn the board.

Backside Turn

 While you are rolling with both feet on the board, lean toward the front of your board. Put all your weight on your toes to turn your board.

1

Manuals are fun tricks to do, but they require balance and practice. The first thing you need to do is carefully push off using your back foot. Then move forward.

2

As you are rolling forward at a reasonable speed, begin to move your weight to your back foot. This should cause the front of the board to rise.

3

Keep adding more weight to your back foot until the front of the board rises.

4

Keep your front foot over the front wheels. Use the tail of the board to balance as you move, keeping the front wheels raised. Add weight to the front of the board to push it down.

Manuals

The **manual**, sometimes called a wheelie, is a fairly simple skateboard trick. The manual **involves** balancing on your board's back wheels. In order to do a manual, give your board a couple of pushes to work up some speed. Then move your rear foot a little farther back on the tail than normal. Now push down gently on the tail with your back foot, so that your front wheels lift off the ground. To hold this position, your back leg should be mostly straight and your front knee should be bent. Use your front foot to control the board and to help you keep your balance. Try to avoid dragging your tail on the ground because you will lose your balance and your speed. You might also **scratch** your board. As you begin to slow down or lose your balance, set your front wheels back down smoothly. Once you get the hang of doing this trick, see how long you can ride in the manual position.

Ollies

When you are comfortable on your board, you can try the **ollie**. First try the ollie while standing still on your board. After mastering that you can try to ollie while moving forward. To start stand with your front foot in the middle of the board, close to your back foot. Bend your knees and lower your body slightly toward the board. Using your toes and the ball of your back foot, snap the tail of the board down on the ground. As you snap the tail, slide your front foot up toward the **nose** of the board and jump in the air. The board should bounce up with you. Once you are in the air, bring your back foot up to the same level as your front foot to flatten the board out. To soften the force of landing, bend your knees. Make sure that both of your feet are positioned directly over the trucks. Keep practicing this trick until you can ollie easily.

The ollie is one of the most important skateboarding moves because it is the basis for many of the more advanced tricks. It can be tricky to learn, and it takes some practice to master.

1

To do the ollie, stand on your skateboard with your back foot on the tail. Place your front foot in the middle of the board. Then bend down to gather speed.

2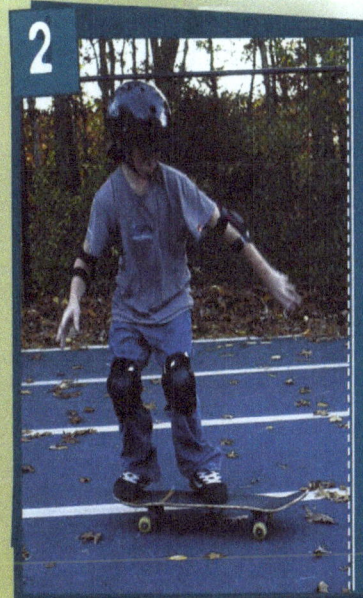

With both your feet on the board, put all your weight on your back foot. Then bang the tail of the board down on the ground.

3

As you knock the tail to the ground, lift your front foot as high as you can. The front of your board will pop up. The back will come off the ground.

4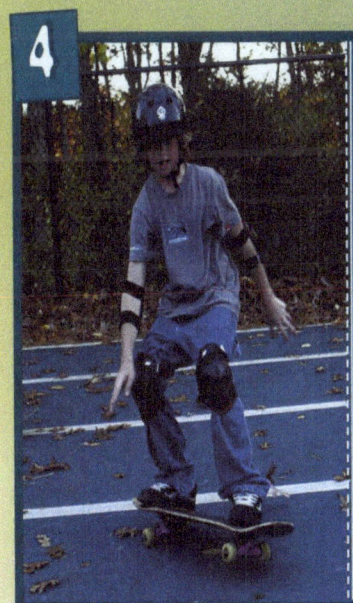

While in the air, move your front foot forward and lift your back foot to the same level as your front foot to level out the board. Land with both your feet over the trucks of the board.

1. The frontside 180 ollie is a hard trick to learn, but with enough practice you will be able to land it! To start move on your board at an average speed and position your feet to do an ollie.

2. Snap the tail of your board down and do an ollie. As you go up into an ollie, twist your body around to face the front.

3. While twisting your body to face the front, move your front foot around as far as you can. Drag your back foot around the opposite way.

4. Keep both your feet on the board the whole time and stay centered over your board's trucks. Land the frontside ollie. You should be facing the opposite way from where you started.

Frontside 180 Ollies

There are many types of ollies and some are harder to do than others. In order to do a **frontside 180 ollie,** you should be comfortable in the fakie position, or skating backward with your opposite foot in front. This is necessary because you will land in the fakie position.

Begin the frontside 180 ollie by rolling along at an average speed. Your feet should be in the normal ollie position, but let your front toes hang off the side edge of the board. Follow the steps from the last chapter to ollie. However, for this trick, as you ollie move your hips and shoulder frontside, or toward your heels, so that your body turns in a half circle. In the air use your front foot to turn the board around. Bring your back foot around to complete the 180. When landing keep your feet over the trucks, stay centered, and bend your knees.

A 180 ollie is an ollie in which you turn in the air. In this type of ollie, you land so that you are facing the opposite direction that you started in, with the other foot forward.

Pop Shove-Its

The **pop shove-it** is a good trick to learn after mastering the ollie. To do this trick, you "shove," or push, the board, so that it spins 180 degrees in the air. Unlike in a 180 ollie, you do not turn your whole body around. You just turn the board. You can "shove" your board either backside or frontside. The backside pop shove-it is usually easier to learn first. To start the backside pop shove-it, snap down on your tail as you would in a regular ollie. After the tail hits the ground, take your back foot off the board and pick the board up with your feet. As the board lifts off the ground, use both feet to guide the board around **horizontally** 180 degrees. Remember, do not spin your body while you are in the air, just guide the board. As the board completes its **rotation**, catch it with your front foot. Then place both feet back on the board at the same time. Land with both feet right over your trucks.

1. After you have mastered ollies, the backside pop shove-it is a good trick to learn. To start move along at an average speed and snap down on your tail the way you would do for an ollie.

2. After your tail hits the ground, take your back foot off the board. Pick the board up with your feet and begin to spin it in a backside direction.

3. Use both feet to guide the board around 180 degrees. This means the board spins horizontally. Remember to spin your board while in the air, not your body.

4. As the board completes its rotation, catch it with your front foot and place both feet back on the board at the same time. Land with both feet right over the board's trucks.

In order to do the kick flip, you have to ride with your feet in the ollie position. Press down on the tail and pop an ollie.

Use your toes to flick the board at the point when the nose begins to curve upward.

This flicking motion will make the board flip as you are in the air above it.

Stay in the air over your board as it rotates. Once the board flips all the way around, catch it with your feet. Land with both feet over your board's trucks.

Kick Flips

In a **kick flip**, you use your front foot to make the board flip around. While you are in the air, the board turns upside down, so that the bottom of the **deck** is face up. Then it rotates right side up again before you land on it. Kick flips take a lot of time and practice to learn.

Start the kick flip by riding with your feet in the ollie position. Press down on the tail and pop a regular ollie. Just as you would for an ollie, you will need to slide your front foot up toward the nose of the board. Then use your smaller toes to **flick** the board just at the point when the nose begins to curve upward. This flicking motion will make the board flip. Stay over your board as it rotates. Once the board flips all the way around, catch it with your feet. Then land with both feet over the trucks.

Advanced skaters make kick flips look easy. However, it probably took most of them hundreds of tries and many wounds before they landed their first kick flip.

Putting It All Together

If you can master all the tricks in this book, that is great! If you can only master a few of these tricks, that is good, too. Unlike in other sports, no one keeps track of which tricks you can do in skateboarding. Skating is fun and not about the amount of tricks someone can do. The skaters who have the most fun simply enjoy the feeling of being on their skateboards and landing the tricks they do know. Of course part of the fun is trying new things. So try to learn new tricks, but always keep in mind which level of skater you are. Be very careful when trying harder tricks.

Now that you do have a few tricks down, try doing them one after another. Whenever you land a number of different tricks one after another, it is called a line. You might try doing an ollie down a couple of stairs, and then snap a kick flip as you ride away. The tricks you do in your line are all up to you, because there are no fixed lines in skateboarding. Just get out there and have fun.

Glossary

backside (BAK-syd) Having to do with rotating in the direction toward your toes.

compete (kum-PEET) To oppose someone else in a game or test.

deck (DEK) The wooden part of a skateboard on which skaters stand.

express (ik-SPRESS) Show something.

flick (FLIK) To move quickly and suddenly.

frontside (FRUNT-syd) Having to do with rotating in the direction of your heels.

frontside 180 ollie (FRUNT-syd wun-AY-tee AH-lee) A trick in which you turn your body 180 degrees toward your heels and then land going backward.

horizontally (hor-ih-ZON-til-ee) Going from side to side.

involves (in-VOLVZ) Is part of something else.

kick flip (KIK FLIP) A trick in which the side of the front foot is used to flip the board.

manual (MAN-yoo-ul) A trick in which you ride balancing only on your two back wheels, sometimes known as a wheelie.

nose (NOHZ) The front part of a skateboard deck.

ollie (AH-lee) A trick in which you fly into the air by pressing down firmly on the tail of the skateboard and then lifting up with your feet.

pop shove-it (POP SHUV-it) A trick in which you ollie and then spin the skateboard 180 degrees before landing.

rotation (roh-TAY-shun) The spinning motion of moving in a circle.

scratch (SKRACH) To rub or tear the surface of something.

swivel (SWIH-vul) Swing.

tail (TAYL) The rear part of the skateboard deck.

techniques (tek-NEEKS) Ways of doing something.

trucks (TRUKS) The metal tools that hold your wheels to the board and make it possible to turn.

Index

B
backside turn, 10

E
elbow pads, 6

F
frontside 180 ollie(s), 17
frontside turn, 10

G
goofy-footed stance, 9

H
helmet, 6

K
kick flip, 21–22
kick turn, 10
knee pads, 6

L
line, 22

M
manual, 13

O
ollie(s), 14, 18, 21–22

P
pop shove-it, 18
push, how to, 9

R
regular-footed stance, 9

S
speed, 17

T
turn, how to, 10

Web Sites

Due to the changing nature of Internet links, PowerKids Press has developed an online list of Web sites related to the subject of this book. This site is updated regularly. Please use this link to access the list: www.powerkidslinks.com/skate/tricks/

www.ingramcontent.com/pod-product-compliance
Lightning Source LLC
Chambersburg PA
CBHW041121070526
44584CB00002B/238